ELLIOTT CARTER

RETRACING

for solo bassoon

www.boosey.com
www.halleonard.com

HENDON MUSIC

DISTRIBUTED BY

7777 W. BLUEMOUND RD. P.O. BOX 13819 MILWAUKEE, WI 53213

First performed on December 3, 2002
at Weill Recital Hall, New York City,
by Peter Kolkay, bassoon

Retracing is excerpted from *Asko Concerto* (2000)

Retracing ist ein Auszug aus *Asko Concerto* (2000)

Retracing est tiré de l'*Asko Concerto* (2000)

Duration: 3 minutes

for Peter Kolkay

RETRACING

for Bassoon

Elliott Carter
(2002)

Con umóre ♩ = 96

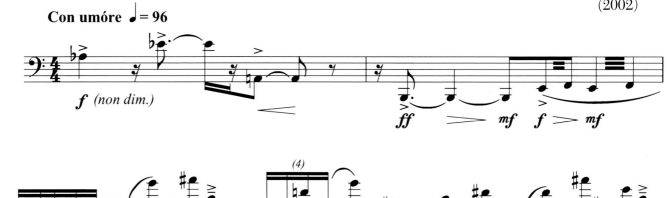

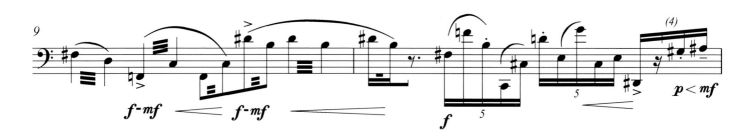

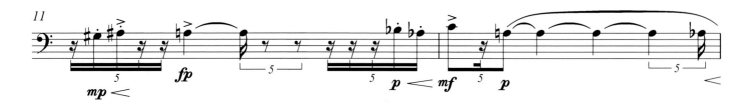

M-051-10451-2

Printed in U.S.A.

Music engraved by Thomas Brodhead